THE
MASON WILLIAMS
READING MATTER

MASON WILLIAMS

Doubleday & Company, Inc.
Garden City, New York

To my Parents
for opening my life

To Ed Ruscha
for opening my eyes

To Tom Smothers
for opening the door

and to you
for opening my book

To be poetic is to bare one's soul
To show all of the holes and patches
Go ahead and step on it
Give it a kick and a Ha-Ha . . .
It'll make it tough

CONTENTS

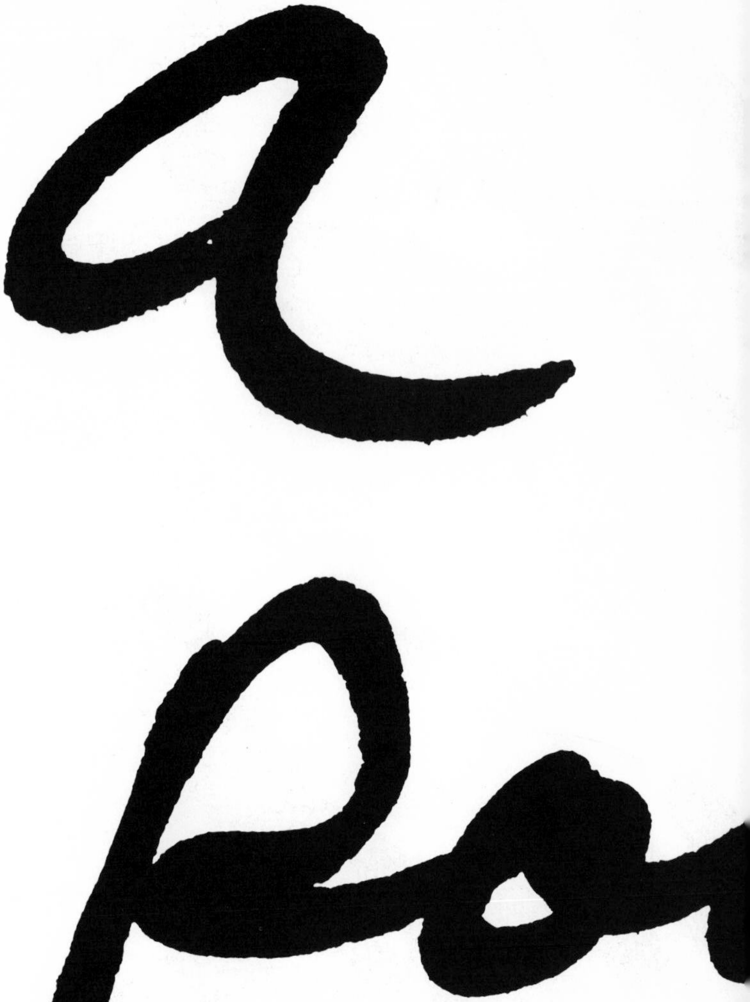

YEP

What's it all about? What's it all about? What's it all about?
it all about? What's it all about? What's it all about? What's
all about? What's it all about? What's it all about? What's it
about? What's it all about? What's it all about? What's it all
What's it all about? What's it all about? What's it all about?
it all about? What's it all about? What's it all about? What's
all about? What's it all about? What's it all about? What's it
about? What's it all about? What's it all about? What's it all
What's it all about? What's it all about? What's it all about?
it all about? What's it all about? What's it all about? What's
all about? What's it all about? What's it all about? What's it
about? What's it all about? What's it all about? What's it all
What's it all about? What's it all about? What's it all about?
it all about? What's it all about? What's it all about? What's
all about? What's it all about? What's it all about? What's it
about? What's it all about? What's it all about? What's it all
What's it all about? What's it all about? What's it all about?
it all about? What's it all about? What's it all about? What's
all about? What's it all about? What's it all about? What's it
about? What's it all about? What's it all about? What's it all
What's it all about? What's it all about? What's it all about?
it all about? What's it all about? What's it all about? What's
all about? What's it all about? What's it all about? What's it
about? What's it all about? What's it all about? What's it all
What's it all about? What's it all about? What's it all about?
it all about? What's it all about? What's it all about? What's
all about? What's it all about? What's it all about? What's it
about? What's it all about? What's it all about? What's it all
What's it all about? What's it all about? What's it all about?
it all about? What's it all about? What's it all about? What's
all about? What's it all about? What's it all about? What's it

I don't know. I don't

There are no empty Tabasco Sauce bottles.

I think it would have been nice to have shared a room with Beethoven and when someone remarked, upon hearing one of his compositions, "Isn't that great!" I could say, "Yep, my room-mate wrote it."

While she was sleeping, I wrote "I love you" on the inside of her left shoe. Shortly thereafter, she went shopping for some new shoes, and the shoe clerk, noticing the inscription, brought it to everyone's attention.

MURIEL WINDOW
Pompano Beach, Fla., Sept. 26.—Mrs. Muriel Window (Turnley), former "Ziegfeld Follies" star who introduced such songs as "Till We Meet Again" and "I'm Forever Blowing Bubbles," died here Sept. 19. She had been in retirement nearly 50 years.

The Muriel Cigar, reportedly was named after her.

CONVERSATIONS

Boy: "Pardon me Miss."

Girl: "Yes?"

Boy: "Do you think that if I wore your glasses I could see you home?"

Her: "It's a lovely night, isn't it? Look at those stars."

Him: "Yes, it is. Say, isn't that a moon?"

Man: "What's he got that I haven't got?"

Woman: "Awareness."

Man: "What's that?"

Wife: "Well, you know the old saying . . ."

Husband: "Yeah."

Man: "Hi, how have you been?"

Woman: "I beg your pardon, do I know you?"

Man: "Yes, we met once before."

Woman: "Where?"

Man: "Right here, as a matter of fact."

Woman: "I'm sorry, but I don't remember meeting you."

Man: "Well, you're a little heavier now than you were then, that's probably why you don't remember me."

Gentleman: "Madam, you have the most beautiful legs I have ever seen."

Lady: "Oh, you're the first man that's ever thought I had beautiful legs. Thank you."

Gentleman: "You're welcome. Mind if I pull your other one?"

Teacher: "Always live life to the fullest, as best you know how and circumstances permit."

Student: "What if you don't know how and circumstances don't permit?"

Teacher: "That's life."

THEM LUNCH TOTERS

How about Them Lunch Toters,
Ain't they a bunch?
Goin' off to work,
A-totin' they lunch.

Totin' them vittles,
Totin' that chow,
Eatin' it later,
But a-totin' it now.

Look at Them Lunch Toters,
Ain't they funny?
Some use a paper sack,
Some use a gunny.

Them food-frugal Lunch Toters,
Ain't they wise?
Totin' they lunch,
Made by they wives.

How to be a Lunch Toter?
Iffa may emote it,
Gitchy wife to fix it,
Go to work and tote it!

RESTAURANTS

Low slung
Modern marvels
Of stone and glass
Sitting on the street
Looking for people to eat
Like architect indians
Scouting the vast uncharted
Frontiers of lunch
Plastic beanery grub mills
Out to kill the appetites
Either by taste or sight
It's like going out to eat
At a hawaiian shirt

CONVERSATION

Customer: "What kind of pie do you have?"

Waitress: "Boysenberry and pumpkin."

Customer: "I'll have a banana split."

Waitress: "Sorry . . . no bananas."

Customer: "Shit."

THE AMMONIATED MISUNDERSTANDING
(A duet to the tune of The Mexican Hat Dance)

1st person: Ammonia! Ammonia! Ammonia!

2nd person: Get off! Get off! Get off!

1st person: Ammonia! Ammonia! Ammonia!

2nd person: Get off! Get off! Get off!

1st person: Ammonia! Ammonia! Ammonia!

2nd person: Get off! Get off! Get off!

1st person: Ammonia! Ammonia! Ammonia!

2nd person: Get off! Get off! Get off!

1st person: I don't mean that I'm on you, I mean ammonia! Ammonia!

2nd person: I don't care what you mean, just get off! Get off! Get off!

30 SECONDS OVER TELEVISION

Tom: "Guess what I'm going to do."

Dick: "I don't know."

Tom: "Guess."

Dick: "You're going to fly."

Tom: "Nope."

Dick: "You're going to dance."

Tom: "Nope, guess again."

Dick: "Alright, you're going to sing."

Tom: "Nope."

Dick: "I don't know what you're going to do, why don't you just give up and tell me?"

Tom: "O.K. I give up. What am I going to do?"

Dick: "Why don't you just go to hell."

Tom: "Nope, I'm not going to do that. Guess again."

THE CENSOR

The Censor sits
Somewhere between
The scenes to be seen
And the television sets
With his scissor purpose poised
Watching the human stuff
That will sizzle through
The magic wires
And light up
Like welding shops
The ho-hum rooms of America
And with a kindergarten
Arts and crafts concept
Of moral responsibility
Snips out
The rough talk
The unpopular opinion
Or anything with teeth
And renders
A pattern of ideas
Full of holes
A doily
For your mind

THEM TUMMY GUMMERS

How about Them Tummy Gummers,
Ain't they dummies?
Havin' they fun
Gummin' them tummies.

Gummin' them paunches,
Outta they mind,
Runnin' 'round shoutin',
"It's Tummy Gummin' Time!"

Look at Them Tummy Gummers,
Lurkin' in the yard,
Waitin' for a jelly-belly,
Catch it off guard.

Them hawn-yawkin' Tummy Gummers,
Ain't they dumb-ox.
Runnin' through the neighborhood
Gummin' them stomachs.

How to be a Tummy Gummer?
No way to shun it.
Grab an abdomen,
Roar off and gum it!

THEM TOAD SUCKERS

How about Them Toad Suckers,
Ain't they clods?
Sittin' there suckin'
Them green toady-frogs.

Suckin' them hop-toads,
Suckin' them chunkers,
Suckin' them leapy-types,
Suckin' them plunkers.

Look at Them Toad Suckers,
Ain't they snappy?
Suckin' them bog-frogs
Sure makes 'em happy.

Them huggermugger Toad Suckers,
Way down south,
Stickin' them sucky-toads
In they mouth.

How to be a Toad Sucker?
No way to duck it.
Gittchyseff a toad,
Rare back and suck it!

A SINGING TELEGRAM

Dearest darling.
You're breaking my heart.
I am a prisoner
For sadness is a pit.
Our love was short.
But oh so pure
You've got to understand
It's you that I adore.
I would be happy
Anywhere with us.
Up in an airplane
Or even in a bus.
If you don't come back.
My future's hexed.
I'm not sure just what
Will happen to me next.

WESTERN UNION
TELEGRAM ®

CLASS OF SERVICE

This is a fast message unless its deferred character is indicated by the proper symbol.

SYMBOLS	
DL	=Day Letter
NL	=Night Letter
LT	=International Letter Telegram

The filing time shown in the date line on domestic telegrams is LOCAL TIME at point of origin. Time of receipt is LOCAL TIME at point of destination

310P PST NOV 26 68 LA243

L BHA106 PD BEVERLY HILLS CALIF 26

DEAREST DARLING STOP YOU'RE BREAKING MY HEART STOP I AM A PRISONER

FOR SADNESS IS A PIT STOP OUR LOVE WAS SHORT STOP BUT OH SO PURE

YOU'VE GOT TO UNDERSTAND IT'S YOU THAT I ADORE STOP I WOULD BE

HAPPY ANYWHERE WITH US STOP UP IN AN AIRPLANE OR EVEN IN A BUS STOP

IF YOU DON'T COME BACK STOP MY FUTURE'S HEXED STOP I'M NOT SURE

JUST WHAT WILL HAPPEN TO ME NEXT STOP LOVE

MASON

SF1201(R2-65)

TOM'S TUNE

I've seen a lot of faces
And I've been a lot of places
So I know I must be going somewhere
The world keeps spinning
And I'm always just beginning to begin
But I never seem to get there
The times and the seasons go on
But all the rhymes and the reasons are wrong
I know I'll discover
After it's all over and done
I should have been a nun

MULL EPISCOPAL CHOICE
(MARK 1)

- ☐ God is love.
- ☐ God is thought.
- ☐ God is God.
- ☐ God is paught.
- ☐ God is faith.
- ☐ God is you.
- ☐ God is all.
- ☐ God is blue.
- ☐ None of Thee above.

ACROSTIC

Acrostic is a poem form
Containing a device
Rhyming's not essential, no it
Only makes it nice
Sometimes it is difficult
To write acrostic muse
It took a lot of patience
Composing this for youse

HOW TO COUNT FROM 1 TO 10
IN SPANISH IN ENGLISH

Who knows
Those
Waves
What though
Sea cold
Said as they
Sedately
All chose
New wave way
Zeniths

THEM DOG KICKERS

How about Them Dog Kickers,
Ain't they crumbs?
Kickin' them doggies
In they buns.

Kickin' them Afghans,
Kickin' them mutts,
Kickin' them puppy dogs
Poor little butts.

Look at Them Dog Kickers,
Ain't they cute?
Some use a shower-shoe,
Some use a boot.

Them dadgum Dog Kickers,
Ain't they mean.
Run 'round kickin'
Ever dog what's seen.

How to be a Dog Kicker?
Don't need a ticket.
Find an old dog,
Haul off and kick it!

THEM MOOSE GOOSERS

How about Them Moose Goosers,
Ain't they recluse?
Up in them boondocks,
Goosin' them moose.

Goosin' them huge moose,
Goosin' them tiny,
Goosin' them meadow-moose
In they hiney.

Look at Them Moose Goosers,
Ain't they dumb?
Some use an umbrella,
Some use a thumb.

Them obtuse Moose Goosers,
Sneakin' through the woods,
Pokin' them snoozy moose
In they goods.

How to be a Moose Gooser?
It'll turn ye puce.
Gitchy gooser loose and
Rouse a drowsy moose!

THEM HORS D'OEUVRES

How about Them Hors D'Oeuvres,
Ain't they sweet?
Little piece a cheese,
Little piece a meat.

Once upon a time there was a man who worked at a job for fifty-two years and never missed a day. When he retired, the Company gave him a dinner in his honor and a gold watch. Think of that wonderous watch—telling fifty-two years worth of time at a glance and also letting him see the rest of it run out.

TIME SONG

What has happened to time?
It doesn't come around anymore.
The very last time I saw
Was a-whistlin' out the door . . .

Sometimes I wish that I were still just a paperboy back in Oklahoma City; where my problems were only thick papers, rain and cold weather, a few mean dogs, a couple of grouchy people, and porches I couldn't hit from the sidewalk.

We were discussing dying and we agreed that if one of us died, the one of us left would be required to write the one of us dead's biography. We both decided that we wanted to die first.

"THESE ARE THE TIMES THAT TRY MEN'S SOULS:"

When Justice is over-ruled by Law
When Peace is attainable only by War
When Freedom is sabotaged by Organization
When God is only a device for Immortality
When Progress is stifled by Traditional Ignorance

And Baby, these are any old time

HOW
TO
DERIVE
THE
MAXIMUM
ENJOYMENT
FROM
CRACKERS

Speaking man to man, the most important element in deriving the maximum enjoyment from crackers is the choice of a companion to help you enjoy them. She must be someone whom you admire. A beautiful woman, elegant and accustomed to sophistication, a woman whose company is a challenge to enlist, a woman that's hard to get.

In approaching the companion that is going to help you enjoy crackers, it is best not to tell her of your intention; let it be a surprise to her. Be charmingly mysterious, saying only that you are going to do something currently different. If she accepts your invitation, proceed in making the following arrangements.

Reserve two hotel rooms for the same night in two different hotels; one a single room in a skid-row flop house, and the other, a suite of rooms in the finest hotel in town. If you do not own an expensive car, make arrangements to have one at your disposal for the evening.

On the day of the occasion, a few hours before you are to pick her up, purchase several heads of lettuce, romaine, endive, fresh spinach, etc.; several pounds of fresh ripe tomatoes, cucumbers, celery, olives, green onions, and so forth. In other words, whatever ingredients you would choose to make an attractive salad. Finally, you must also purchase five gallons each of the following dressings: Roquefort, French, Russian, Thousand Island, and Vinegar & Oil.

Take these ingredients to the room at the skid-row hotel. Pull back the covers on the bed and make a four or five inch layer of salad that covers the entire surface of the bed, tossing the salad well with your hands. Pull the covers back over the salad and re-make the bed. Be sure there is no salad on the floor. Place the twenty-five gallons of dressing in the closet.

With the above accomplished, proceed to dress for the evening. Dress as though you were a waiter or a wine captain in an expensive restaurant, but leave some doubt as to whether or not this is what your attire really suggests. The doubt is, of course, a personal matter. When you are dressed, and all of the necessary arrangements have been made, proceed to pick up your date.

When you call for her, create an air of wistful mystery. However, try not to make your mystery dark and ominous; keep it light and taunting. If she asks you what is planned for the evening, it is very effective to look into her eyes, smile faintly, but saying nothing, and then look away.

Drive casually to the flop house. Make interesting conversation; keep her wondering; answer her questions about what you are going to do with only, "You'll see."

When you arrive at the flop house, take her quickly to the room you have rented. Once inside the room, ask her this question: "By the way, what salad dressing do you prefer?" When she has told you, go into the bathroom and drape a small hand towel over your forearm (a la fancy waiter). Return to the room and pull back the covers on the bed to display the crisp green salad.

One of the high points of the evening is now at hand. You must coax her to lie down in the bed. She may possibly reject such a notion at first, and may even attempt to leave. Reason with her adroitly. One of the finest points of argument to convince her that it is perfectly all right is "salads are good for you." If she is still hesitant, you can even go so far as to chide her for not being adventuresome. Whatever you do, get her in that bed; get tough if you have to, but get her in that bed!

After she is in the bed, go to the closet and take out the five gallons of her choice of dressing, and with great flair, pour it over her entire body. She will probably make some remarks like: "What is the meaning of this ridiculous tableau? Are you mad, you crazy son-of-a-bitch!" Enjoy them.

When you have emptied the entire five gallons of dressing on her, snap your fingers and say: "Crackers!" Begging her forgiveness, explain that you have forgotten the crackers. Tell her that you will have to run to the store, and for her not to move a muscle.

Race out of the flop house, drive swiftly to a store and buy a small box of saltines. Do not buy fancy crackers. When you have purchased them, drive to the fine hotel in which you have rented the suite of rooms. Go directly up to your suite, place the box of crackers on the nightstand beside the bed, take your clothes off, and get into bed. Turn the lights off, settle down, and nibble on the crackers one by one. You will derive a maximum enjoyment from them.

LOST
AND
FOUND

we can't rely on his good
or bad intentions - He eats
a little and flops.

If Chi - Chi - Continues her
pattern, will take her to
the place for breeding tomorrow
She was out an hour, early
Friday evening - found a boy
friend and was almost
hit by 2 cars — so don't
know how many lives she
has left.

Our very best wishes -

Love,
Lil

Bill is O.K. -
didn't feel too
good last week
but is real good
today.

Arden & Rossmore
Hollywood

Norton & Curson
Hollywood

THE EDGE
OF THE WEST

To begin with
The sea is a sound
A down and around pound of sound
A lot of swish and splish
The smell of something big

I went down to the Sea
Bearing a garland of words
To honor the Sea and the Night
The Wind and the Stars
And forgot them in my passion for sea shells

Don't go down to the ocean
With a notion
Of what you will find

LITTLE TOY SHOVELS

As little toy shovels
Are lost by the sea
So are the children
Like you and me

DAWNSEA

In the early morning moonlight
I cast my net into the dark horizon
And the dawn
Like the gleaming belly of a surfacing fish
Leapt from the sea

FOURTH OF DECEMBER FOG POEM

Fog whistles
Far away
Mooing like cattle
As the night
Dissolves in watersmoke
The Sea comes in
To look around
Disguised as
Mr. Fog

I am amazed at the total lack of beautiful young women
dressed in sheer negligees on the beach after ten o'clock at night.

TO TOM'S BOAT
"THE MORNING STAR"

All dressed up
In a white wind catcher
The morning star and we
Shall set our hand
And soul together
Upon the rolling sea
Away beyond
The edge of the West
Where all of the distance rhymes
And only the sunlighted day
And the moon-mirrored night
Survey the tides and times

TUESDAY NIGHT BEACH POEM
27 NOVEMBER 1962

The Sea
Whose myriad tongues come
With sea-stenches, drenches
Spray-tossed edges
Whose lowest voice shouts
Death-breath gusts
Of life's longest loneliest ballad
Whose splendid winded waves
Weariless mysteriousness
Go on and on forever

FAIR
WEATHER
POEMS

SKY COLORS

A deep blue sky
When seen
From around the corner
Or from behind clouds
Is County Fair
And the glowing whiteness
That follows the wind
Is obviously another day

SUNSET COLORS

A great flowering sunset
One where the sky is green
Foretells of yellow rain
A sunrose
Red with clouds
Flowers later in the morning

FROST

The first draft of winter
Is usually etched lightly on
An early autumn dawn
With extreme prettiness
Reaching well into
The falling horizon
Occurring more often
Until perfectly snown

FOGS

Settle down the weather
And that stuff is fog
Good mornings
And good fogs
Break up before noon

HALOS

Sun dogs lay
Around the sun
And bark in rhymes and runes
Rhymes are fair
Runes are rain

RAINBOWS

Rainbows are ribbons
Of light fantastic
Tied to the rain
Before and after
Bows in the morning
Before
Bows in the evening
After

THE
SAD
TRUTH

WINE

I am from the finest of jewels
Those upon the vine
I drank of the dew and the rain
Ate honey of the sun
And so my flesh was this
I was gathered
And my sweet blood flowed
To await the bitterness of time

I am the taste of loving
In the lover's mouth
I nourish the joys
And sorrows of the heart
Of all who approach the fire

RIVER

I am born in the sky
The silent snow is my seed
In the season of the sun
My crystal blood runs
Over the earth
Gathering unto itself
Godspeed

Whispering in the beginning
I uncover brown and gold
Yellow, red and green
From under the whiteness of my mother
Until I have voice enough
To carry leaves
And roll little stones

Warmed by my father's touch
I gather the strength
By which I am to live
And hasten further away
To where I am abundant

In pools where garlands of grass and leaves have fallen
I have fishes and tiny miracles
Some drink of me
And I sustain them
Reflecting their image in my lifeblood
Like a swift mirror

I bear the colors of the sky for my banner
And make a path for the wind
And fog for the night
And mist for the morning's meadows
And rainbows when I soar in cataracts

I have ferns and rushes on my edges
Hardrock and towns
I eat away my earth-sides
And color myself in it
I rush and roll and roar
In white plumed manes
Like a fierce stallion
And sing and glide
In greens and blues
And run the deep silence
To meet my brothers and sisters

We blend our bloods and soils
And fishes and voices
To carry boats and big logs
Our strength is harnessed
And we are painted and photographed
Marvelled at and swam in
And given a name

We flow over dams and under bridges
You pour honey and oil and sewage
Steel and dust and paper into us

Spent and sullied
Slowly we go on down
To be lost in the sea

A STONE'S THROW AWAY

I must have thrown
A billion rocks
When I was a kid
I had more time
Than I needed
So I threw it away

The spinning stone
Is a moment thrown
The distance tossed
Is the moments lost
The kid alone
Is good at stones

in
the
unroamed
loamed alone
of cathedral forests
where resounds the
echoing silence of the
great organ timber pipes that
tower into the crystal distance
among the cool green and
deep honey dark secret caches
of shadowed silence there grow
the christmas trees
child trees still suckling
woodmilk from beneath the moss
to lift their sapling fingers and touch
full stride their miracle
but these child trees as christmas
ornaments are severed from sanctuary
by seasoned hunters with steel saws and
shiney axes and brought to towns
priced and tagged trimmed and dragged off to
christmastreetion camps where amid
the pallor of neon and the roaring ugliness of the
christmas crash they wait for christmas
people to inspect them and select them to fit a
certain space in a certain place so much
less than a wilderness with tinsel and glass paper
and plastic trash foam and fuzz flashing lights
and icons they stand dressed to hide their slow dry dying
M
E
R
R
Y
CHRISTMAS

WOODY GUTHRIE

Hard man born of hard times
Lean and leathery wanderer
Seeker of songs of the sun and the earth
And the hand and the heart
Poor proud poet of the working man
Ballad maker of the dust bowl days
Singer of Victory Songs
Singer of Brotherhood and Peace
Singer of America's silence

DYLAN THOMAS

Dylan Thomas
    Has come and gone
Come and gone
    Come and gone
Dylan Thomas
    Has come and gone
His blood
    Turned to words

DEATH

You will know me by my touch
It is the last

TO WHOM IT MAY CONCERN:

TO WHOM IT MAY CONCERN:

I want to billow
In your thighs
The sweet havoc
To burst beautiful
A moment in you

Girl: Look at all you've given me tonight. You took me to dinner, for a lovely walk, wrote me a poem and made me a bed of rose petals. I haven't given you anything, have I?

Boy: I wouldn't say that. You gave me someone to eat with, it was a nice night for a walk, I write a lot of poems anyway, and it was a chance to do something else with flowers.

Girl: Then I guess we're about even.

Boy: Yeah, I guess so. 'night.

Today, while washing my clothes, I saw a young couple leave the laundry-mat together. The woman was pulling a little laundry cart behind her. They smiled at each other and the man gave the little cart a little kick.

Soon you begin to realize that "I don't want to" is the world's greatest reason.

That day she dove in the swimming pool and I envied the waters' ability to touch her totally.

I was really bored sitting alone in my motel room, so I jumped up and went to a restaurant and had some shrimp and apple pie, a glass of milk, a big bowl of chocolate and vanilla ice cream and orange sherbet with chocolate syrup on it. On the way back to my room, walking beside the pool, I saw the table where the two fat men and the lovely young lady had been sitting earlier this afternoon. Their beer glasses were still on the table, so I went over and touched the handle of her glass.

Getting in bed, I cuddled close to her good leg.

WANDERLOVE

Come my love and we shall wander
All of life to see and know
In the Season's lostward rambling
All things come and all things go

We'll climb up the snowy mountains
Sail across the rolling sea
We shall live for one another
I for you and you for me

We'll go down to green grass meadows
Where the cold winds never blow
If we taste the wine of loving
Only you and I shall know

Come my love and we shall wander
Just to see what we can find
If we only find each other
Still the journey's worth the time

Love is like a star of heaven
Burning in the endless sky
When it falls it bursts asunder
As it lives, so shall it die

HERE AM I

As the universe spins
To a desolate end
In the Doldrums of Destiny's Sea
So should I accept being
As reasonless as
The firmament's futility
. . . but here am I holding your hand

As often I've thirsted
So often I've tasted
My fill of love's honey and wine
But in desperate drinking
The savor of loving is lost
And so never was mine
. . . but here am I holding your cup

In a garmentless promise
Of nothing we stand
With only the raiment of time
It is ours to endure
Or endear and end up
Embracing whatever we find
. . . and here am I holding your mind

LOVE ARE WINE

Love are wine
It tickles my mind
And I'm
Always got drunk
Evertime
On love
Oh how life fizzes
In fact
The whole world is
Real good
When it whizzes
Along
On love

Ladies is grapes
I are feet
When togathered
We're complete
We make wine
The sweet kind
And it feels
So fine
Just to get
Stoneblind
On love

Pretty love
Turtle dove
I'm thinking of
Lovely love
The kind you shove
Up your soul
And feel a whole
Lot like
Red roses
Look

Love are wine

LOVE POEM NO. 2

Come to me
Do not hesitate
I am not funky

Please be mine
Let our hearts entwingle
Like honeysucker

Jump around me
Scuff my boots
Fingerpoke at me

Skippy-toe by
With owl-growls
And Fa-la-la's

Love with me
All your grits
As I love you

WINDOW

I turn sun
To dawn
Upon you
A radiance
To light
Your prisms

Your eclipse
Across the fire
Masks the
Sun reigned
Naked night

I sleep warm
Beside the embers
In the window

TALKING A BATH

I liked that,
Sitting on the bathroom floor,
Watching you take a bath,
Talking to you.

I stuck my hand
In the water and slowly
Moved my fingers along
The softness of your thigh.

I took handfuls of water,
Spilled them over your
Milk and silken shoulders,
Enjoying the gentle
Sensuousness of your skin
Slick with water.

You had your hair pinned up
In lovely disorder
To keep from getting it wet.
And you played as you talked,
Little splashes
With your fingertips.

Talking a bath,
I liked that,
And I don't even remember
Anything we said.

SATURDAY NIGHT AT THE WORLD

It's a Saturday's night at the world
I am thinking about a girl
And how useless to search it becomes
When you seek all the answers in one

But her voice seemed to answer the echoing silence
From yesterday's asking
And waiting and listening
For something resembling a song
To be sung back to me

And her eyes seemed quicksilver
Reflecting the prisms I kindled
Uneclipsed by the darkness of loving's mirages
That swindle the heart
With the shadows of we.

And her love seemed to offer a sojourn
From endless beginnings
So I went spinning into her
To love her, but found her
One answer for loving and losing the same

It's a Saturday's night at the world
I am thinking about a girl
And how useless to search it becomes
When you seek all the answers in one

TOSADNESSDAY

Today's not the first
Nor the last
Nor the best
That you and I have known
The first never was
The last never will
The best may have come and gone

I'm not the first
Nor the last
Nor the best
To ever have loved you so
If the first and the last
Have come and gone
The best you may never know

Love is a journey
The moment it begins
The journey's all it is
No matter where it ends

ROAD SONG

... and there, just outside of Rush Springs, was a fat girl, tap dancing on the highway . . .

We were riding along in the car on a plateau in Colorado, going to Aspen. We saw something up ahead on the roadside. It was an Eagle, the symbol of American freedom, feathers rumpled, standing in a dirty patch of snow, hitch-hiking.

. . . and just around the corner, there, lying in the street, dead, with baby-seat agog, on its side, a supermarket basket, killed by the wind . . .

Is a car windshield a "windshield" or a "window?" Is the primary function one of "to shield from the wind," or is the primary function "window?" Is the fact that one can see through a windshield secondary to the shielding properties?

. . . and by the way, where are all the tons of rubber that have been worn off tires since cars began?

I woke up and looked at my watch. It was 7:30. It was hot and stuffy in the little room. Sweet Suzie, last night's lady, was asleep beside me. I layed there for a moment, thinking about a cold white glass of milk. It seemed like the purest thing in the world; one sip could wipe out the acid memory of last night's honk.

I eased up out of bed to dress. My shoulders ached, and though I couldn't remember carrying anybody piggy-back, it was not improbable.

I dressed, and opening the summer screen door quietly, stepped outside into the patio. I didn't see any sign of life, but I didn't see any sign of death either. It was too early for anything, the sun was only shining in the tops of the trees. The cantino across the patio was dark, but I tried the door. It was locked.

I walked around the edge of the patio, looking for a way out, but the walls were high, and as if that weren't enough, the tops were embedded with jagged pieces of broken bottles. The only possible way out was a bright red wooden gate. It was locked, but there was no glass or barbed wire on top of it as far as I could see. However, it was about twice as high as I was tall, so I walked to the far side of the patio, opposite the gate, turned and ran toward it. I jumped onto the middle of the gate with one foot, glancing upward, and grabbed the top and pulled myself up. I made a lot of racket, and I remembered that there was always a Policia at the entrance of the cantino. What if he were there now, or heard me and came running to investigate? What if he shot me, thinking I was a thief? What if he thought I was trying to get into the whore house? He probably wouldn't even consider the idea that I might be trying to get out. People would read about it: "A young man was shot and killed early

Sunday morning, trying to get into a whore house in Nuevo Laredo, Mexico." What would I say in my dying breath to explain? "I—I was just going out for a glass of milk."

I finally clambered over the gate and jumped to the ground, sprawling in the dust and gravel as I hit. There was no one around, so I ran to my car, got in and drove off.

On the way back to America, I drove past a junk yard; a man there was working on some automobile tires, pounding on them furiously with a big hammer. God, I thought: "What if, instead of escaping from whore houses, I had to get up early and face a bunch of dirty old tires?"

Border Inspector: Your nationality?

Border Crosser: American.

Border Inspector: Are you bringing anything back from Mexico?

Border Crosser: No.

Border Inspector: Any fruit, perfume or liquor?

Border Crosser: No.

Border Inspector: What's in the trunk?

Border Crosser: Nothing, just some junk.

How long has it been since I've been somewhere
Somewhere that's more than something to see
How long has it been since I've been somewhere
Somewhere that means something to me

I've traveled roads in California
Winding along through tall shady trees
Read all the signs from Maine to Oregon
Though they were not meant for strangers like me

Way out across a field of cotton
A farm house light shines like a star
The road doesn't turn, it just keeps going
To some next town that seems so far

I've made my way through valleys and mountains
Walked through the bushes, sat under the trees
Rode the dark miles in trucks and buses
I never cared why—my reason was me

How long has it been since I've been somewhere
Somewhere that's more than something to see
How long has it been since I've been somewhere
Somewhere that means something to me

I'm on my way

LIFE SONG

Isn't life beautiful
Isn't life gay
Isn't life the perfect thing
To pass the time away